LIFT EVERY VOICE

ALSO BY PHILLIP B. WILLIAMS

POETRY

Thief in the Interior

Mutiny

FICTION

Ours

LIFT EVERY VOICE

PHILLIP B. WILLIAMS

PENGUIN POETS

PENGUIN BOOKS
An imprint of Penguin Random House LLC
1745 Broadway, New York, NY 10019
penguinrandomhouse.com

Page 83 constitutes an extension of this copyright page.

Set in Birka LT Pro with Arima Madurai
Designed by Sabrina Bowers

LIBRARY OF CONGRESS CATALOGING-IN-PUBLICATION DATA
Names: Williams, Phillip B. author
Title: Lift every voice / Phillip B. Williams.
Description: New York : Penguin Poets, 2026.
Identifiers: LCCN 2025049505 (print) | LCCN 2025049506 (ebook) |
ISBN 9780143138860 trade paperback | ISBN 9780593513002 ebook
Subjects: LCGFT: Poetry
Classification: LCC PS3623.I5593 L54 2026 (print) | LCC PS3623.I5593 (ebook)
LC record available at https://lccn.loc.gov/2025049505
LC ebook record available at https://lccn.loc.gov/2025049506

Printed in the United States of America
1st Printing

The authorized representative in the EU for product safety and compliance is Penguin Random House Ireland, Morrison Chambers, 32 Nassau Street, Dublin D02 YH68, Ireland, https://eu-contact.penguin.ie.

CONTENTS

FERVOR

RECUMBENT

PARADISE

PSYCHOPOMP

LIFT EVERY VOICE

AIDE-MÉMOIRE

Bones sing to water the crowded graves.

All elegies the elegy before: break and cycle.

Elegies water the graves and crowded bones.

Break the crowded bones and the graves sing.

Sing: graves, water, bones. Elegies water

the cycle. The crowded graves break to water

before the water breaks the cycle. Before,

elegies crowded the graves. Sing the before-

bones before the bones break. Bones cycle

the crowded elegies, cycle the crowded bones.

Graves break, elegies. Sing to the crowded graves

before the bones break water. Sing the crowded

water bones. Elegy, sing the bones to break

the cycle. The cycle: Sing to break. Break to sing.

FERVOR

REFLECTION ON DUST AS FORM

An artist friend depicted Romulus and Remus as onyx
boys suckling from a two-headed sapphire dog: one head

in the back, one in the front. Truth and lie dog. East
and west dog. Dog of split allegiance. Dog of mirrors

that reflect only sky, sea, or sorrow. Predator
pressing forward and prey watching its back. Dog

of looped hunger. Of coming and going, and past
and present and what difference will it make? Remus

nursing at the west should say it all. The way history ends
is how history begins. Nectar from a hunter confuses

the game. The twin black lips purse toward oblivion,
which is heaven shaped canine. Their tight afros brush

the dog's underbelly. The heaviness of storms,
an unkindness of ravens in the thick of augur.

And the blue dog has dozens of nails driven into it,
as though to hang small paintings of air

from its body, or crack it open to the nothing-organs,
or awaken what rested inside. Is either boy, or dog,

or the entire enterprise sculpted as an empire
to last in? My friend pointed to one nail puncturing

back out from the same side of its entrance.
She said while hammering in the nail it curved

itself against entry. Said a hard presence must be inside,
harder than a betrayed heart, which I find impossible. *Resisted*

is how she described it: The interior resisted the injury.
One brother resisted the other and gave the wound

his own name—called it home, called it power, called it
the howl that competes with itself, nurturer of murderers,

a protracted suicide. The point is to allow entry. Let everything
that has tried to break you get inside. Allow the nails

their destination, allow the rain to hang from your steel eaves.
Allow the wielder his work, even if the hammer has your face.

WHILE READING AI

on the train, an ashen-skinned man squeezed his junk
while watching me turn the pages. His pupils rolled
to the back of his head as he bit his chapped lips
for a taste of fresh blood. I watched him watch
my fingers, stiff as pocketknives, scan through killers
who felt more like kin. I licked
my right index to smear the forehead of a rapist,
turn one page to smother a Nazi only to find more
drowning in my oily thumbprint. Yes, I became
vulgar, seeing in him the poet who had entered
my dorm room one summer among other poets.
It was night. Night has a way of proving you right.
I hated him then and hate him now, the poet
who strode toward my bed, permissionless,
and I had to push his sweaty power off me
and out my door. When I locked the door, he knocked.
Imagine that. The audacity of a failed thief.
Sometimes, without warning, a man can change
his mind, can gladly become the putrid muse.
That train rocked one good time and my face
shuffled through its better selves
behind a billboard's fleeting shadow. Understand,
I go greedy for what I am
owed. Every version of me wanted a turn.

WHITE BATH

Because I was dishonest with my request,
instead of love I was sent a lure, and look
at what lurks in the low—his curt face, so sure
he's unsure, so fallen he rises against it
to our detriment. My dreams were full
of lures: waving stingers, imagined cities that loved me
vulgarly, a life of touching skin and the warmth
demanding endless want. I remember hugging
his flinching body, and the streetlight flickering
a ghosting warning. One time too many,
a man wanted me so bad he stalked my dreams
but wouldn't return my calls. Broken-
hearted, I went to porcelain-hugged water
to drown my grievance. I listened to the running
faucet flood my hollow life, the liquid
blessed into gasp and applause. Who or what
waited for me in the mason jar filled with holy
water, Florida water, rose petals pale
as sympathy? Ground eggshell fogged up
my future. The water's steam rose like hands
to obscure the mirror I saw less and less
of myself in. Brokenness led me to this perfume
and sweetness: Confused, upended, the contents
pooled, dispersed, then floated around
my submerged grief. I found rose petals
had settled at my feet. A garden can grow
even here? My voice surprised me
as it bellowed in this sudden sanctuary.
"Walk with me, Lord," I sang and placed
those petals that were once my steps
over my eyes to see the path, submerging
my body beneath the bone-tint water
to breathe for the first time.

WHILE READING HENRY DUMAS

bones begged to be read in the dream
about reading the bones, cascarilla-colored
catfish spine cutting the human throat that cries
the divination caught supine on the scry-
scattered dirt. What is the color
of tomorrow? Dreaming foretells the dream.

THE HEAD OF GOLIATH

David with the Head of Goliath (1610)

And like Caravaggio, I am my own savior
rent by my own hand. Depicted:

A younger version of the painter heeds
his own benevolence, having made lantern
of his older self's unbodied head, meaning even
disappointment may light the way—tenderness
bearing the blade, being the blade—though no light
may touch the wholeness of either, face
halved same-side by darkness, as though the past
bears repeating.

I too have appraised my future and thought, *All this time*
on my knees, for this?

The position of prayer is also one of power:
giving it away, taking it, taking it back. I am one
with my body despite being of two minds
that this life allows such agency. In the distance
the kingdom that is my new life expects my old life
to surrender. Watch as I carry back by its crown the proof
that it can be done. My beheaded blood stains a trail
in the sand, unnoticed except by my younger self

who will return to that place to admonish himself
for what he has done and prepare for what he will become.

MORRISONIAN

In seven days, the procurers of doom
will kneel in a mound of velvet petals,
rose-red plumes. Patient ancestors make room
beneath tragic men flight lifts then settles

into the perfect snow. White won't last here.
Not in the casket of a guitar's hold
that is a boy's eyes carving into fear.
Not in the pile of men in piles of cold

drawing vèvè with their barbered hair. Once,
there was a story where stories refused
to barter with the tongue. Now a bright fuse
has lit a path from canon to the blues

to the heavens, a fusillade of wings
Chukwu-bound, the people could fly, my God
it's brighter in August these days. Let's sing
that the worshippers of doom will see how God

said "Good" after seven days and ended
their reign just as quick. These blissed August days,
these rivers belching black dresses mended
to evening. Let its billowed malaise

be token for my mother, dream augur
who knew seven ways to say *bitch* under
her breath, as though singing underwater
to the children whose chains still glow down there.

Now hear her singing: "Children, children, go
where I send thee, and how shall I send thee?"
Her dead brother's shoeprint in perfect snow.
Her dead father's soft laughter in the breeze.

Tragedy! Tragedy! Those who love ghosts
summon ghosts in the mourning, troubadours
of salt. Griots gathered our names from boats.
Bones became Psalters on history's shore.

My mother's brother died, intestines curled
in a bag. Charlie Parker blew robins
from his record player. Black vinyl whorled
into a world he could downright die in

and where did he learn how to myth himself
free, giggling at me, his guts in a bag?
What gives this life its lore, fiction its breath
like a breeze of laughter from my dead dad?

Is this the paradise that never comes
but through the lilies' rot, an empty dress
or ribbon in a river—skin undone
in its bow? Is this the promise of flesh,

that it will break clean like a ghost-thrown dog
and still stay put? Still in this paradise
retrograde in certain countenance. Fog
unspooling from my coal-skinned uncle's eyes.

My father disappeared in rocks of snow,
his wan face blade-carved in a violet tone.
Can a man be a burning dress that knows
the Devil's silhouette? A bag of bones

hangs from my memory like an earring
in servitude to gravity. I kneel
in a house of a hundred dogs hearing
the one bell for the End of Our Days peal.

All four grandfolks deceased, my grief standing
like horses standing like men fugitive
into dusk. What chapter speaks of branding
"love" into a corpse that cannot love? Give

Shadrach to fire to learn the failure
of fire. Some folks die to keep others
from dying. My mother saw the future
and still made a family. Ancestors:

By the book's end everybody is dead
serious in the makings of love. See,
there was a novel in my mother's womb,
and in my unborn throat there was a sea.

WHILE READING *SULA*

I realized I was Nel and wept
for the robins rotting inside me. I had not borne snakes
or roses made of cinders. I rose from bed
bored, snaking my way beneath
ashen men child-hungry
and respectful to thieves. I refused to fuck
because I was no votive. Why should I burn
while a man mumbled
Christ—scared—above me?

THE THIRTEENTH AMENDMENT

"Negro citizens, North and South, who saw in the Thirteenth Amendment a promise of freedom—freedom to 'go and come at pleasure' and to 'buy and sell when they please'—would be left with 'a mere paper guarantee' if Congress were powerless to assure that a dollar in the hands of a Negro will purchase the same thing as a dollar in the hands of a white man."

—Jones v. Alfred H. Mayer Co. (1968)

From here on out, what is owed is pleasure
bleeding from an allegiance, the pleasant
scent of the hatred of things. A pleasant
privilege *no* is, "not this one, nor that." Please,
Black joy exits the room for Black pleasure.

I don't have to be happy to be pleased,
my eighth house crowned in sunlight. Pleasantries
aside, mystery fortifies the pleased,
leaves something aching to be found. Pleasant?
I'm anything but. Will leave unpleasant

parties to less pleasing company. Plead
with God, not me, for a better life. Please,
I never asked to be born, dear, but please
know that, born, I'll do what the fuck I please:
make vellum of my skin for needles, pleased

by my own face tattooed on my face. Pleased
to meet me, the pleasure is all mine. Please
excuse this mess, or don't. Or, can you please
see yourself out? I bought back my bones, pleased
with a life soft as a tissue ply. Sure,

shame in the shape of me haunts my leisure,
but "My liege," I say in the mirror, "please

don't cling so hard to innocence." Be pleased
you can be more, no "see me, please!" no pleasure-
less pleading. I'll build a school for pleasure,

make a revolution by displeasing
the pleasure-broken, the people pleaser.
No pleasantries. Just fire. Just pleasure.

FOLK/LORE

Wipe your red lipstick off the rim of that glass. Who
    you tryna hex? Somebody getting rode in a game
of spades, them cards coming cardinal make a hard
    divination. Don't walk round no whispering trees.
Don't walk no loop round me. Don't turn round
    in the mirror. You won't know who looking back.
Coins collecting on the armoire, moved but never removed.
    Penny for your thoughts. A dime a day. A quarter
past twelve they gone circle back and see who home.
    A clapping game between four children, double
Dutch a recurring eclipse, what's above now
    what's below, stomping the ground, calling the names.
The Electric Slide faces four futures and never ends.
    Somebody Black won the 400-meter again. Grandpa Black
puffing rings of cigar smoke. Cousin on kush.
    Ring around the rosy, all around the mulberry bush.
Wedding ring on the dresser, initials in the band.
    Boy, I'll wring your narrow neck with both hands.
Don't ring my bell; just come round back. Shape
    that baby head till it make sense in the back. Don't
yawn with your mouth open. Don't roll your eyes.
    When the wind blow it blow a wreath, west
to east, bringing the dead with it, karmic orbit
    as they swing back, red dusk arcing into red dawn.

WHILE READING *THE ORCHARD*

a six-headed stag casts a strict shadow
in my mind where moonlight is the only light.
Umbra of reach. Umbra of letting go. The stag
bows his six chins to open his closed bud of horns
into a single crown, into a weight that can hold
nothing inside. It holds nothing, not even air
that is so easy to hold and not hold. When the yellow
moon arcs bright overhead, the stag's shadow
stretches over the stiff grass like an engorged timeline.
Umbra of measure. Umbra like a puddle
the stag could sip with its six heads, black water
falling from the mouths. The crown's shadow draws
sharp points, a tree of every family the moon
has ever seen, a father and mother at the tip
of each branch. When the stag heads tremble—it is cold
in the mind—the fathers and the mothers tangle.
I got my sister that way but, in that story, only
our father swapped branches, our mothers as frozen
as the one stag head that has ceased moving, dead now
or sleeping while the others turn to the child stag,
turn to the brown, white-spotted fawn, to the hornless
thing lying not far off from the stag
and his many heads with mouths leaking dark water
as would breasts leak milk, warm dark water
that the fawn has never drunk and the water
dripping down to the stiff grass in the yellow
light of the moon. The brown fawn has found itself
a bed of roses to rest in. The roses' thorns cut
into the fawn, cut flesh into red mouths
dripping blood to the soft grass, the sound
of blood on blade like the sound of rain in a field,
the scent of iron out of place outside
of the body, iron the scent that signals predators
to come with their hunger. There are no fangs

here. It is pain that eats the young. The fawn licks
blood from its thorn-pricked legs, hair slicked down
from the thick-wet fawn spit
the moon cannot make a mirror of. The fawn
stands and its own shadow lies down,
stubborn-like, a contradiction, while too the roses lie
still warm and unfolding the way a crumbled man unfolds
from a dream that has crumbled him, for what is buried
in his dream has tried to come out but failed,
this time has failed. Was his face the face my sister saw
in that other story, a face she would never see again
except in a mirror, a mirror in which she looked
for herself but only saw him? What could he feed her?
There is water in his veins. He nods
without sleeping, dreams of thorns making mouths
in his arms too small for his famine, the smell
of warm metal, the scent of rose-red blood.
And now the fawn stumbles toward the stag.
Their shadows mix as the fawn on branch-thin legs
walks to the dead or sleeping head that has not looked up
for some time and licks the muzzle. What if
that stag head opens its eyes and lifts
its chin, opens its mouth at a speed so slow
it deserves a sound, though there will be no sound
except from the tremble of the stag's many heads,
their thick horns clattering, the crown shattering?
If the branches reconfigure again, their source
a beast, would hidden kin bloom in the cold
to feast on water, on shadow, on the nothing air?

PASTORAL, NOTWITHSTANDING

The poplar knows the edge of voice and permits hiding
in its shade. The magnolia holds what is holy close
to its darkness. The boughs no more a fear-traced
remembrance (oh, the fire there, the swinging). Yes,
bless the roots and the kingless crown beneath which
the fugitive may hide their balm and blade. Beyond sound,
the way wind wears the leaves speaks the ineffable.

At the edge of skin and silence, at the meeting
between secret and lovers, initiatives carved into bark,
symbols arrowing toward deep abandon, the clearing
out of noise for the clearing to flower freely. Light
broken up by branches falls shattered to feet fleeing
the light. Let willow shade work away the work.
There is sleep to be had in this marronage dark.

THE LENGTHENING AND SHORTENING OF SHADOW

I.

Formidable, the light
dawn breaks across the field
of our vision is stationary.
We revolve
around our own potential
seeing. The tree knows
nothing more is needed
but stillness and rise,
rootwork and praise
as boughs branching out,
caught in light,
catching light,
splay their near-human
ache skyward, scratching
the commands of God
into the falling light
in a language we cannot read
though we see it etched
angular like prophets struck
by heavenly vision, trees
the first worshippers, leaves
of shout and rebuke,
the roots testifying beneath
what the living foliage
holds up till, living-dead,
the tree freezes in the one
sound that is God's
many names announced
in the wind,
though we hear only wind.

II.

Earth spins like destiny
in a clock's incessant
instants. Time
is no linear kingdom.
Starting east, birth.
Then counterclock-
wise to noon, middle age.
Old age in the west,
sunsetting unbelligerent
in wise folks' eyes
as the wizened body
goes down to the root,
down to the ground-
water, down to the death
of death. Of course,
Christ came back, lifted up
on the cross that is arrested
time, a tree in final frost
waiting to return,
waiting for the sign.
How any father waits is how
his sons thereafter wait,
circle then converge, patience
an inheritance, spiral,
settle, and blossom.
The father always
comes back so the son
never dies. Eternal
lesson, a boy searches
his Bible for evidence
that every father leaves
his son a useful sacrifice,
a blood memory,

a yoke for the exiled dog
that warily walks forward
while hungrily looking back.

III.

I took the sun's hand
and its bright heat to heart
while learning how
to backflip in my father's
mother's garden, wild
strawberries surrendering
their minute organs
to our appetite in due time.
But for now, my father,
his hand on my back
as I bend back, build
a bridge from my fear
to his, half circle birthing
my sonhood and his fatherhood,
the wound and salve
touch predicates
in a memory old as I am
now, he then likely the age
I am now writing this,
his hand on my back
a keystone, trust
ripe between us. I thought
that was the beginning
of family, that man
letting himself father
me. It astonishes
me into love to see
him that way, helpless
as he builds a tomb
for himself with my body,
holding me near inversion,
we evidence of each other, gilded
in afternoon, suspended, me

stuck in his grip,
in his specter
as helplessly—don't
help me—I am now.

WHILE READING LUCILLE CLIFTON

my father visited me
while wind turned its nightly pages
and his grave gave purpose
to the movable earth.
his smile careening through
past and future summoned me.

I answered my sonhood furious and a man.

seeing at once all four corners of his life
I remember him despite myself
flirting with rage. I no longer believe in
the worst of my father. spoons
let go their heat. in his hand
his reflection right side up and singing.

WHILE READING MELVIN DIXON

the air in the room went cold with loss.
Another man I needed to know gone

into the null light. Here was legacy,
chances deranged by blood and zodiac.

I had come to find some navigation
for my grief, to find in its stars some trace

of family. Generations sickened,
my mentors haunted the banquet of ash

and could not eat. I wanted scrutiny
and a head rub, but the dead were tired

of my uncrucial nostalgia. Then he,
a man I didn't know but felt I knew,

materialized like tobacco smoke,
like a newborn god naked as a stone,

calling himself "Uncle," and I believed,
calling himself leopard king then he screeched

from the table's far end and stomped his feet
on the two and four, made a flame stammer

from the skeletal chandelier and drop
to the table for which we had no seats.

Fire caught the curtains till their vague curves
expired. The windows of our madness

dragged up for a god-holler of vast wind
to caress us deep into our first selves,

stricken with moss and salt, while in our white
attire, dust anointed by our feet took

ancestral liberties. Uncle yelled "Now!"
to the storm plunging its jewelry into

the river till its vein constellated
ellipses leading to a golden throne

room of masks and confession. I followed
Uncle's instructions, his machete wet

with harvest: "Remove your damn shoes in here.
Lift your head like the hot dawning coin lifts

green from frost. Your pennies dull. Your arch flat.
Your red candle weeps cold smoke. Nephew, what

illicit moths chew through your ego? Burn
your mojo for seven days. Powder your

doorway like an ancient locksmith who guards
our original, formidable names."

RECUMBENT

A STRANGE AIR DRAWS NEAR

"Oh mother, mother, where is happiness?" —Gwendolyn Brooks

Know the dead will not come back.
Begged or bargained with all night,
Nothing reaches through the crack.
Nothing breaches left or right;
Rules apply and stay in place.
Even prayers draped in lace
Won't allay internal lack.

What dispels internal lack?
Decimating living will,
Issues issued come in stacks.
Prayers stuck on windowsills.
No, the dead will not return
Brandishing their swords and urns,
Shields of dust to take the slack.

Troubles trick and turn about,
Demons of a mind ill-eased.
Trusting too much too loud shouts,
Glossolalia diseased.
Doubt defines the unredeemed.
Churches fill with churning screams,
Living-dead feigning devout.

Mother comes to make amends.
Father's face holds rotting time,
Never husband, sometimes friend.
Caskets soften temporal rime.
Alchemists, morticians work,
Bringing solace to mourners
Skeptical this end's the end.

Mother says she saw this come,
Prophet in her own high prime.

Father dead with just a crumb,
Nothing resembling a dime.
Feels his forehead with her wrist.
Virtuosic surrealist
Hoping fever's soon to come.

Home is where her weather falls.
Hidden sorrows find their crest
Knocking down her fort-forced walls,
Disregarding kin and calls;
Nosy neighbors waste her time,
Questioning if she knows best.
Blessings curse from mouths unblessed.

Now we have to let her grieve,
Choir still inside her ear.
Chocolate cake frosted with tears,
Funeral then wake then seethe.
Know the dead will not come back.
No, the dead will not come back.
Still, the strangest air draws near.

ALL IN LOVE IS FAIR

Stevie Wonder (INNERVISIONS, *TAMLA RECORDS*, 1973)

I. Father

He forgets   to be there   is hard

        earned   displacement   of a hand

when you hurt   the debt

        by not paying   soon enough   mother wanders

where you cannot   follow not   even   in a dream

        does he know   now that he is too late   to see

where   does he look   where his eyes can't   rest

        the world keeps moving   without her   there   is no future

II. Mother

She remembers   his first love   is music

    where he lays   his head   depends on the heart

keeping up   with him   nothing is for certain

    when she opens   her eyes   unable to see

through the windows   in his arms   she thinks   unsafe

    thoughts   that never kept   a man who runs

from thinking   the junk   makes things better

    between the two   of them three hungers   can't make a home

III. The Junk

got a howling in it that make a howling pool

beneath the skin. Another version

of self historicizes

the previous versions into fable. *Them fools was never*

me.

Just like music to say that

every other take was another song

altogether. Folks be forgetting the art

that is true composition,

to find a more comfortable truth. Need a little blood

to come up. You was always

music. First the needle pulls

the song out,

then it puts the song in you.

TOO HIGH

Stevie Wonder (INNERVISIONS, *TAMLA RECORDS, 1973)*

before this swift life goes four-eyed monster
a flying white lady wearing China white
with gumption gets your calcified third eye
to cozy the mangy carpet brown-sugared
with vomit and red drip that is not not a pillow
but good-gahtdamn the couch right there, Boy.

couch a big H, a wide-chested boy to help and hold
before a fastball snowball beheads you upside
the table. concussed and cussing. red. volatile
as Hera kinking as white nurse ladying up the wares.
body shape settled in the carpet. sugar-crust-lips-like
but just a three-way spill drying out the shit talk

spilling out three ways: piss, blood, and prayer.
gahtdamn couch coughed you up, no hero.
body shaped like a suicide that won't go, carpet
head-heavy holding an upside-down
sleep. wake yo ass up. white horse wearing you out
and why red-red where you sleep, man? black eagle

sleep in your arms' spotty red. what method
you pixelate with? pointillist pops praying from sixty
mouths, not one on your damn face. white nurse horsing
around all gahtdamn and church cough. heron balance
for the kill. fish see bird head holding sky upside down.
ceiling light god-shaped. no carpet in heaven

for you to lie on your god on. somebody in heaven
found you, though, unslept you for another red day
and thank goodness they fished you out yourself.
pressing digits. your mama pick up praying.

dragon calling you on the other end. damn, hero.
white nurse a white lady in China white on a white horse

saying “save me, Black. help me, Boy.” white
lies don’t work on your mama or your god.
a need smack into you and you just different. damn
who found you fucked up and tell them thank you.
tell them call your mama again. lips press mouthpiece.
the goodness of fish. white bread that multiplies.

getcho ass up. carpet vomit mean a new day. outside
snow a white-white unholy, whole block screaming
gahtdamn gahtdamn gahtdamn gahtdamn gahtdamn!

ALL IN LOVE IS FAIR

Dionne Warwick (Live in Cabaret, *1975)*

Mother

I tell you our son can sing like you he has found everything
can fall away and be reborn on the inside our son
had to rebirth himself our son needs you appear today
smelling like yesterday a fear that you will run
again with a promise of return not even the wind
is the same wind blowing back into town you guilt or guillotine
shame or requiem brother what is your name is
not in this house you are not in this house we make room

~

come home   make a home   here   is the door
wide enough   your addictions   slip through   the keyhole
won't allow your rusty key   access to your son   you want this
love that won't burn   though the chemical kiss kisses   beyond
doubt   never stopped you   before   you gave yourself to Christ
the God within   fought   the god within

~

ever seen a man howl   at the sun   you threw   your voice
I didn't know   I couldn't compete   because I didn't know
there was another light   infidelity the least of it   the most of it
slow-dancing behind your eyes   many rooms you made   in your mind
into one room   the glazing ache   for escape   I can't speak to
what needs spoken to   you hide your hand   and the rocks
you throw   yourself into the arms   of deprivation
you know   a beautiful feeling smiles   inside   you   rot while standing

THE DIFFICULTY OF DESCRIBING LONELINESS

"real madness came / That day shadows began to cast people everywhere"
—Bob Kaufman

Shadows peeled themselves from the ground and laid
flesh flat against concrete warmed by the flesh,
against grass petrichored into potion,
green gabardine of blades etching into
human writhing. Shadows stepped dark-up into
the sun, erected a statuesque void,
looting light. They dragged skin across asphalt,
traced blood like fresh lipstick on mirrors kissed
narcissistically. When they made love, we
thinned into nothing between them. Nothing
is lesson. Parasitic, my shadow
frustrated my voice into extinction.
Folks saw me and wondered what wound wandered
my body entire, what veneer shone
in place of the face they had before thought
little of. I lay thrown onto the wall,
splayed, a haunted marionette watching
my shadow animate Holy Ghostly
like candleflame whipped by a closing door.
My shadow writes in a shadow's language,
a codified nothing the shade of shade.
Left me mute on the drywall. I mouth names
of loved ones, hoping someone reaches out,
though they'll feel my warmth and still not believe.

SCULPTOR AND CLAY

Mind of my mind, my dead father asks why I make him
live in the fictions of young men who become
mist and dust when they lift their heads. He is trimmed
by their failures. He demands prayer and a second

life. Fiction. I speak of young men who become
afterlives in my hands, irredeemable versions of one
failure. Father declares, "Prayer and sweet rum
won't clean the tarnished altar you left me, son."

Afterlife in my hands, irredeemable versions of one
hellish heaven that won't even let him through.
I won't exalt the tarnished altar. A left-behind son,
I craft my father from death's hue.

Heaven, I won't let him enter. I helled him into
the faces of fathers who can't keep promises,
crafted fathers framing death's hue.
They lurk in this terse dirge. My blunt silence

my father faces is a well-kept promise.
I can't imagine a grave he won't drown in,
looking up from cold dirt, his blunt silence.
He begs for forgiveness, for me to free the men

I imagine him drowning in. A grave he can swim in:
mist and dust. When father lifts his head, I trim him.
He begs for forgiveness, but there are no free men
in my mind, my father the answer to why I made him.

ALL IN LOVE IS FAIR

Nancy Wilson (All in Love Is Fair, *Capitol Records*, 1974)

The Junk

I sleep in excrement
voices the gift mute
unregulated I came to father
born bound in absence.
Skin a peeled dominion

when I came I came familial
noses took in this new
brother OD'd a father
house after house skulls
licked white

I was committed
to reason what was
rumor time
father left pliant
return I could return and turn to

hustle a deal
flipped
through an anemic
catalog white-jeweled
coffins

father veins laugh
time a face a crater
mouths labor dust
the white horse hoof over hoof
the sour horror

I most brilliant force
forced
folks
off their knees prophets
that see their own decease.

be capitalism no no
be Devil white
affair
hostages
love this God-fear.

I an allegiance
with I incredulous light
the city of teeth curses
I arrive element and
hollow

addict the trees
poltergeist
the moon braids
light shakes
dies

I kiss
a bouquet of
blunts entrails
burn in reverse
baby this a place

of worship a messenger
the blooming tongue
father
carrying his falsetto
in the

losing   run away fast
lung inscriber eyes
coaxed   inward lacking
a mind cavity heirloom
an erotic   pain

blood weave   nests haints.
dear rot   razor   a body
bare smile   endless   lake
reflection   re   flection   keep
the locket closed   eyes dear father

dear   dear   I

EPIPHANY

What if every boy
inside my work isn't
me in any version but
is my father waiting
on someone to see
the boy he
unlikely got to be?

*

Even when violence
violates the boys'
interiors, makes abandoned
homes of them,
my father stares from
their shattered windows,
haunting the haunting.

*

In his obituary, my father's
last name is stitched
to mine, though his name
does not belong to me.
I was loaned my father's name
after he died. I was loaned
the sky then told to look down.

*

Father, you were so kind.
Do you understand,
now? You were
so kind to me

as I borrowed you
from your habit,
from the hug that harmed you.

*

I heard tell loneliness
keeps addiction near,
and addiction keeps
loneliness close, a charm.
One makes the other
make the other. The cycle:
Sing to break. Break to sing.

A HOUSE IS NOT A HOME

Luther Vandross (NEVER TOO MUCH, *EPIC RECORDS, 1981*)

Father: a tenor so a beggar, a man who knew
the rain and that in it he belonged
pining, sky-stretched arms, *baby-babying*
another baby into a woman, another baby
into a woman, another baby, etc., eventually to—me.

Who got the body, my dead father's,
a jones a ruckus inside and hearable
even now if my ear to grief serves
better than the ever-absent body
his fatherhood, fled from me, fell into?

Thus a choir was made, I too a tenor
failing singing to sleep a father wound.
Listen. Flutter-hum. Flint hymn
that is need and abandon sparking
alive in the blood an unloving pleasure.

Who kept my father's runagate feet
callousing to and into his last breath? Who
found him breathless, a still-warm finale? I
am his encore. I know addiction's taste, my
drug my own mind against my mind's

sprint toward proof it can withstand
its belief: No one will ever love me, no lust
-warm hand or kiss, haint-cold. Was my
father's body as cold as my mind or still
warm as his paraphernalia glistening at his feet?

Who found my dead father, and was he smiling,
fogged out in ritual, a ceremony crucial

to my desertion? Did he remember
me in his too-high high? I miss him, one-winged
apology, Saint of the Thin Wounds, and mine.

When my father died, I dreamt of him
in the recesses of his mother's garden, wild
strawberries ruby against his fickle hunger.
Then the deathlight lit absurd with blue.
I pray he was found, a pietà on the couch,

deathlight-lit, an absurd blue. Bible open
on his chest to Corinthians before sliding
shut to the floor, and I hope he died with love
anchoring his heart, his heart a flung-open
door that in death I may finally enter.

Crossing over this side of peace while I
cut across the static blood of him, stalled
heart, grief mine, his name in my ear echoing
from his four chambers' surrendered rooms.
I cross his heart. He crosses over Jordan.

Deep river. Deep river that is his body crossing
over, crossing over. My father has crossed on.

CASCADE

For all the fatherless children, the lake's bottom.

For all the children butchered by abandonment,

make them somnambulists in heatless nights.

Give a sleepwalking boy a lyre of wind and a score

he can't read. Rest, I tell my legs as they march

to the tune of a night terror toward the black

wet's call. I'll go in as flesh and come out

as water falling from the bowl of a pelican's beak.

DON'T PLAY THAT SONG

Aretha Franklin (SPIRIT IN THE DARK, *ATLANTIC RECORDS, 1970*)

To the father who missed the only bus
within the harsh hour that would get him
to his daughter's recital on time, luck
his main antagonist—a boss
who delayed him for a minor infraction,
a car whose engine seized up
in the parking lot, the ATM that only
had twenties and the cashier who had
no change, a gas station ten blocks farther
closed because of a leak, then the next
location half a mile away, and the final
timely bus turning away from the empty
bus stop where he should've been.
By the time the next bus arrives
at his destination, his daughter is near
the end of her song, had been staring out
into the semi-dark, clenching her white
church dress and scuffing one black shoe
with the heel of the other. She wonders
if she has missed him in the mosaic
of faces blurring oceanic behind her
tears, somehow the one barrette
come undone and clinking to the floor,
somehow the stage lights hotter
by the passing second, the song more
difficult to complete, so she waits for him,
pretends she has forgotten the lyrics,
looks back at the pianist who smiles
encouragingly for there is only one
verse left darling then we're done
and can go home but she does not
want done she wants fermata

stillness handless clocks one
more song one more barrette a cooler
dress a softer microphone a home
somewhere in the eyes of someone
already there who had been there watching
the entire time mouthing the words
with her saying her name saying "Yes,
baby girl. Keep going, Pooka! Sing!"

PARADISE

PARADISE

"I was once nothing and then suddenly I was fixed"
—McKinley Dixon, "Beloved! Paradise! Jazz!?"

Let there be light and Leontyne Price
singing "My man's gone now," lion-
throated, the Met a gala of stars

trembling golden light
over her star-studded shoulders,
her gown a galaxy, her arms

a gallery of dripping light, light
filling the cracks in beauty with beauty.
Her voice sealing a broken world

with a song about a broken love, dead
man gone to violence, a dying opera
gilded by a golden voice. A son looks

for his father in that song but finds a dope
dealer dusting a front porch like a priest
sprinkles salt at the front door to keep

evil from sliding through. Golden eyes
peer from the dope house window,
sealing the cracks in the glass. Everyone

deserves a life of loving on the love
of their life, deserves diamonds
dripping from a lioness's ear. A vibrato

of trembling stars shakes free of dust.
"My man's gone now," a roar, a confession
making a lesion in the legion of loss.

Even here in the cup of her voice
cusping sorrow and wrath, a man
who's formed a habit curls into his woman

and shakes wings free from his back.
First, the skin bulges then cracks
into bleeding, letting a bit of golden

mucus seep through. Then the primary
feathers black as a hurricane, a fuss
of rusting blood rushing up, stretch

from the fissures. All God's children
got wings and a ring of gold
round their throat. Let a man sing

of beauty met up with blood. Let a man sweat
and shake a bit, withdraw into the night
of his woman's star-flecked arms.

A man just wants to be useful as a broken
fix fixed with the hold of something warm.
Let something warm hold him and hold.

This is how you rebuild somebody's daddy.
This is how you mend a house with gold.

PARADISE

"And at that centre, with their wings expanded,
More than a thousand jubilant Angels saw I,
Each differing in effulgence and in kind."
—Dante, *Paradiso*, Canto xxxi, translated by Longfellow

Angels dream in cocoons and when hatched
are named for their dreams: Falling, Sleep, River
Fish. It's painful and bloody when they grow
their wings and they grow their wings in fever. In Heaven

a nightmare could follow you forever and forever
you'd be known by what you fear: a child
named War who dreamt of a burning field,
Love who dreamt of waking up alone.

The angel named Nostalgia dreamt of dreaming
they could speak only in the past tense,

their present already occurred
as it happens; their future always behind them,
which in retrospect fit
the future, as a king, believing
an unacquired territory is already his,
secures the territory.

Sun Tzu said, *If at a great distance from an enemy*
of equal caliber, do not pursue battle
because exhaustion will be yours
in the presence of a refreshed foe.

But the king, by speaking, had accomplished,
already, the crossing nearer to.

Is that faith or arrogance mistaken as
destiny, the untoppled tower imagined as ruin
thus ruined, the not-yet-burning soldiers afire?

There was a distinction I'd mistakenly created
between infamy and renown, the mistake

of giving murderers a name—the Zodiac
Killer, Jack
the Ripper, a birth name
with the ink not yet dry—that seals their immortality.

My little angel, a woman says
to herself in a mirror
in a dream, her angel name

Abandoned. In Heaven, one can be in Heaven
while on the way there. One can be there
and never pass the gates.

Nostalgia said, *My self has died*, and
in a great and endless confusion, flexed
their wings. The wind

has blown, is blowing, will blow—

PARADISE

"I'm yours / You're mine / Like Paradise"
—Sade, "Paradise"

Assassinate the stars by granting time is ersatz
brutality, a lover awaiting a petal bevy
come down from its "loves me, loves me not." Cicatrix:
dead river carving its phantom dune. Moonbow:
echo of light haloed in a curve of light, an improv
fulfilled between source and refraction. You
ghost through lovers' lives then steal the evidence, abet
haunter and hunter to grow from a paramour's
inquiry. Where did you go, abandoner,
jester who staggers, who staggers a stuttering heart? Q:
Kill the stars by counting their living-dead days or stop
loneliness one wish at a time? A: You too
may stay yet scar, may false start toward one wan
night. No nova, just no one. Arm
or armory, both hold potential harm. In a newborn's caul,
pulsating quasar. In your adult disguise, dwarf star, struck
quarry for blood or blood diamond. Your path no hajj,
records instead prints gone remiss in your tread, and I,
shallow follower, found a farther figure in your fallout, ash
traced into human shape God blew no breath into. Fog
unfurls where last you stood. My knees scoff
veering off all fours, crawling from the cave
where you are both shadow and caster, forged
xanthic day just torchlight and whim. Sun is a relic
yawning from the past. Heaven is a vacant tomb,
zenith of a heartbreak stretched alpha to omega.

PARADISE

"How many of them are you and me?"
—Stevie Wonder, "Pastime Paradise"

If I remove myself from this world maybe
others would live a better life. If I was ash,
not soft resistance, fallen light without endless
attempt to rise—

Every dime in my coffer annihilates
a people. "Did you sign the petition?" Who doesn't

already know the options will never
know. Solidarity is sacrifice,
is the end of comfort. What you want
in this lifetime you will not stop your spending for.

Every cell phone a genocide. Every latte
a border redefined, a chronic removal
of trees. There will be none left
of the things we love at the swipe of a card.

Social anxiety makes me paroxysmal
at the protest. What has this country done to me?

"Did you sign the petition?" Did I kill
my appetite for convenience? Does nothing,
having nothing, becoming nothing resolve
the smoke? Have my taxes fed a grave

today? Is there such a thing as hope that is not
eventually weaponized? What is silence
if not blood, but over there?

What has this country done to you?

Books were not first to be banned.
Was flesh. Was water. Was land.

The line grows long with exile and at the airport
for a murderous cup of joe. Everyone
suddenly a master at war. Receipts explode
a hospital, funds a militia coated in coltan.

There are millions dead at the tip of my thumb.
My motherboard sourced from a mother's destruction.
Don't look away. Not yet, as you live to look away.

In a relentless whisper, my cowardice says,
"Admit it,
the destruction of others makes you
feel safe.
Then you must accept your destruction
brings peace
of mind to another person in this world."

Don't look away. Don't look away in the now or ever.
It is the fear of death that has made us dead.

If you believe, feel free
to skip this part: Your life
is death. My life
is death. The easiest sleep this side of civilization.

An ancestor's wildest dream—

PARADISE

"Love has a playful heart / That's where the hatred starts"
—Rufus featuring Chaka Khan, "Fool's Paradise"

—while up the street, a boy has been shot
while buying Pampers for his twins. Try

to understand where we are. This is not
anywhere new, or particularly dangerous.

There are two fathers here: one, bleeding
by the automated door that won't stop

opening behind him like an impatient
heaven; the second, holding a weapon

that's suddenly too heavy to hold,
the weight not at all like the small weight

of his son's hand in his, but maybe lighter
than the envelope holding the medical bill

for his son's treatments. You'll have to
imagine the ailment to fall in love with him

enough to shoot someone who wants
the same thing you want: more time,

and for the blaring music and the greasy
funk of wrinkled hot dogs and the bleach

stink leaking from the mirrorless bathrooms
and the screams outside and heaven's

dinging bell and its glass gate closing
halfway then reopening as if confused

by the man who won't enter the light
to all stop. See? This indefinite plight?

There are two fathers in love. I am trying
to make it make sense, the trembling

hand with the gun and the trembling hand
stopping blood with a fresh Pamper,

the bleach fumes, the boy's weeping
wound, and the gun's barrel in my eyes.

Heaven in my ear now, the bell bright
and the entrance light harried by beetles

a lesser poet would call angels but, baby,
I am good at what I do. It's just now, I'm not

sure where to go, or how I got here with all
this weeping, all this waiting, all this love?

PARADISE

"Thou art my Father, thou my Author, thou / My being gav'st me"
—John Milton, *Paradise Lost*, Book II

1.

A close friend tells me my mother told him my father
committed suicide. Not how overdosing works, love.
My father was trying to live. Every day he was absent
from my life, he was deeply attending his own. Music
made my father. I tell myself he was teaching himself
how to play the guitar. Why else pluck each vein note
by note? The music was inside, love, and like an artist
obsessed with his craft, he couldn't stop. His falsetto
matched the pitch of his blood. I hear that musicians
are magicians too. Could you find the right chord
on the first try? That was his problem: A brotherhood
of sound was in his body. Every damn note was right.
There wasn't enough time to show me, so to keep
from dying in my arms, he turned himself into a song.

2.

Part of my training as an HIV tester and counselor
was mimicking how heroin users cook and inject.
It was strangely familiar, the part where the strap
hugged my arm and my blood rejoiced. That I could
throb that way. Even now I hear my stiff pulse
push and stall. Memory makes that kind of love to you.
The smell of the strap is the smell of hot latex. Inside,
my blood demanded hooves. Strange to want the animal
so close. I envisioned a needle flooding a stampede
into me. Did my mouth water? Did my father's?
I know whose child I am. I don't know all the men
I could become. Unwrapped, my arm stopped yearning.
I kept myself from smiling. I look like my daddy
when I smile. I look like him when I'm asleep too.

3.

Speaking of my father's addictions, I imagine my own
and come up betrayed as a pair of hands open
after prayer. Nothing nested inside my kissing fingers,
no womb where baby Jesus wails from or grown
God groans out His good advice. So, my addiction
is to zero as an empty promise is to self. I am not suicidal,
but I am in endless wonder as to who will miss me,
casket closed tighter than my corpsèd eyelids flickering
for a peek at the loudest mourner. My father's body
never touched my sight. I sat near back of the church
determined not to make the first move. If he wants to,
he can, even in death, make a way out of no way.
Is faith always this weightless, a hand nobody can hold?
I pray. My own hands touch. My own warmth answers.

PARADISE

"How exquisitely human was the wish for permanent happiness, and how thin human imagination became trying to achieve it."

—MISNER, FROM *PARADISE*, BY TONI MORRISON

We read about war and wonder
where weeping goes. We look for a sign.
We are out of rain, so we reach for fire
and find the excess startling. We find prayer
in the balm of a bird's flight, teaching us the wind.
We find flowers and know they are worthy.
We find Darwish's hymn in the horseman's heart.
We put it in the heart of a child
and the transom between day and night cracks and falls
at our feet. The child wakes
to eternity birthing in the sky a sign: rain and fire
at once. Eternity at the feet of a child.
There is more time. There will be a harbor, a home.
Home—may your feet know the softness of stillness and pollen.
Home—here, the stones will not betray you.
Home—your body is yours, your body is yours and is yours.
To the cruel days behind you, we say melt into eternity.
There is enough darkness here to shade a generation.
To fall in love beneath. To sleep within
its weeping. The bird's flight startles
like a sudden bell at the end
of prayer. At the end
of prayer, how does life begin?
How flowers begin: a seed, a breakthrough, a bud
opening as if to chant, "Like this! Like this! Like this!"

PSYCHOPOMP

'TIL EARTH AND HEAVEN RING

And here begins the impossible lift
no narrative should undertake as ev'ry
vein in me down-plucks into a voice
like an akonting punctuating a tale and
preparing the air around it to sing
about my father's mother till
I get it right, till I understand the earth
wanted her mind, her stroke-struck mind and
got it. But let me begin first with heaven
meaning heaven's location is the wedding ring
looped gold around my grandma's finger, ring
that I imagine because when a child with
eyes that examined ghosts more than the
people who feared them I missed the harmonies
that were two rings throwing back the light of
the television while my grandparents watched Liberty
Mutual commercials, holding hands. Let
us begin there, in the space between our
handholding as I take you toward rejoicing
that these two were married in the rise
of Civil Rights to the impeccable high
of addiction that slipped into aunts as
a bottle and uncles as everything else, the
world marrying my people to a listening
cruelty that overtook the earth and skies
with the slow burn of spirits and syringe. Let
us begin with spirit. Let memory embalm. It
won't hurt until it does. Memories resound
like the chime of two rings tapping, loud
as a mind struck by lightning twice as
a blood vessel bursts twice, the
scroll of a life unrolling and rolling
from my grandma's impenetrable eyes, their sea.

Imagine a ring finger off-balance, the sing-
song cling of two rings kissing now a
hushed covenant a fist makes of a song.
In hospice, the bed lifts and lowers Grandma's full
weight, her eyes like two open books: Book of
Quiet, Book of Wind. Light bursts behind the curtain the
stroke placed over her stare. Have faith
she's still there, and I do, I believe that
voice in me that trembles like her hands the
truth of the matter: She knows and has tasted the dark.
My mother says my name, says I am there past
the veil, past the peculiar curtain a blood burst has
dropped between us. Grandma stares like my name taught
her how to see again. She cries. Curtain lifts. Now an us.

Grandpa said the first stroke made her sing
against the floor, her body dancing to a
flamboyant tune only she could hear, a song
made of every song she'd ever heard, full
life coming to birth all at once, all of
a sudden, the choral interruptions, the
sonic boom of Mahalia Jackson's hope
interpolated into Al Green's wail, that
hybrid of God and *please* and doubt, the
higher ground of Stevie Wonder present
in memories of her own hands touching, has
to be for the Lord; she loved the Lord who brought
her thus far. An everything-at-once He has brought us.

The second stroke stole language, thief facing
us from her open mouth, squatter in the
gasp, her voluminous moan rising
like an empty shirt blown full in the sun.
The second stroke stole control of
her body, hence the hospital bed bending our
recollection of that home, a new place, a new
cryptography to study, how night and day
merged on my grandma's tongue, had begun
to break logic itself in that bed. Let
me begin again. The impossible lift. The narrative. Us
holding hands as I take you where I cannot march
to alone, though I was not alone on
that journey, my younger sister there too, smiling till
she started looking like Grandma, a victory
like resurrection in real time. What is
family if not the fact that we had already won?

I'll tell you this and believe me or don't: A stony
look overtook Grandma as she gripped my hand, the
strength of a livid woman, and through her eyes a road,

through her tears, permission, and I promise you—we
have a long way to go—that I was made to trod
into the portal of her grieving a still-lived life, bitter

but brilliant, her shucking this still-life shell, the
path opening before me, chastening
me who had trusted words more than flesh, now rod

in stone for water, thread in the air to catch light. Felt
we were going someplace she had known before, in-
capable of seeing her world rise in her on my own, the

horizon a plucked banjo string, days
sprinting from her into me, atemporal genesis, when
tumbling into when, into wind, the hope

in a bowl of grits and catfish, her unborn
daughter pushing palms to belly. Had
I not seen it for myself, had I died

the death of a dying fancy, I wouldn't yet
believe the spell azaleas cast with
their clustered blushes, the hoodoo of black pepper a

quick hand drops. Safety soon and steady.
Then I'm in the car with her, beat
by spring storms sliding into summer. Have

mercy, the Chicago River's drawl cares not
for our impatience, its length making our
journey to hospital echo Exodus. Weary

the hours exiled from hours, days of feet
becoming miles, one home gone, the other come
close, like a promise, like a menace, to

a place slick with lake water and smoke, the
place of greystone and riot, choked place
where the hand around its throat is its own. For

now, I return from my grandma's past, which
mythic with contour consumes the present, our
knowledge now resumes in minutiae: Fathers

and mothers, what prayers have you sighed
watching your children become your parents? We
never thought the genius of love would fall, have

not yet defined the genus of this loss. I have come
embossed by premature grief made mature, over-
whelmed by this adult cradle in the living room, a

casket's cold exhibit displaying the way
toward future graves. I feel Grandma's fixed grip, that
hand that she beat me in dominos with.

I don't deserve to see this memory. Tears
betray because here, post-stroke, she smiles. Has
it been that long since I've been

without myself that I couldn't see me in her, watered
into a sulking garden, a heredity, cells of we
woven into an I who favors her son? Have

I fallen into loss and become loss? Come
tomorrow, what tomorrows disappear? Treading
through a book of photographs, I will know our

bloodline beyond memory. Outside the foot-worn path
at a friend's family outing, I found a chewed-through
rabbit's leg, its body gone, bone from the

shin down, a shock of fur around the paw, blood
dried into a maroon crust at the broken tip. Of
this discovery, I think the missing body made the

leg, bent frozen in escape, worth it. Slaughtered,
what good was an articulation without end, out
there, a predator digesting the organs of

a no-longer-whole to remain whole. But here, the
leftover leg was enough to imagine the rest—gloomy
with sullied snow and alarm—sprint past,

an image of the dead repeating till
it becomes another life. I am a broken now
built from a broken before. We

can keep going if you'd like. This pattern smothers. Stand
here a little longer with me, because at last, at
last, I can say she has died. At last, so have I. At last.

At the funeral, Grandpa was the last to leave. Where
else to go? His son had died last year from an overdose. The
pallbearers had fewer hands. White
gloves garrisoned the casket's limits, gleam
where a gleam grew grandiose along the golden edges of
September's overcast. Our
duty: to remember. The sanctuary bright
with lamentation. Everyone outside except my mother, star
pupil of heartache, and myself in the hall. Is
this when I share how my grandpa knelt and howled, cast

out his monstrous grief before Grandma was carried out? God
transfiguring his throat into animal or Angel of
Nothing More, incomprehensible bellow, our
soft-spoken papa mocking death's creaking door, weary
before his dead love of decades, years
hollowed out by explosions of blood, God
tearing space asunder and Job no good, a blare of
the first of seven trumpets and the six thereafter, our
own hearts gone nova from the sternum's locket, silent
no more, an ovum unlocking a lesson born from tears.

The impossible lift: to forgive flesh. *Thou*
knowest, Lord, the secrets of our hearts. Who
stands shocked that life takes from who has
most to learn? All four grandparents dead, brought
through death's sieve by age, cancer, stroke, grief. Us
versus life, we beg for reprieve. Thus
these obituaries shake by candleflame. Far
from gone, they tremble on the altar, on
anointed wood doused in Florida water, the
playing cards face up predict the way.
I'll find my healing in the mud someday. *Thou*
most worthy Judge eternal, suffer us not, at our last hour . . . who
knew Grandpa was an elegy? Death has
made lonely deaths a legacy, a feast by
which we fork and knife our sobbing down. Thy
will be done. That bestial sound might
haunt me always as my grandpa's cry. Led
to the river, I drowned in the river. Us,
we, ours—mistaken generosities. Into
reverence I buckle my knees. The
millstone of loss lowers my neck. Light
be my witness, I know the dead by name. I keep
the river of their syllables cheek-close and warm. *Us?*
Us? Us? Family folded in forsythia, forever
the sun-bleached obituaries curl their corners. In
my bereavement, I kiss their portraits. The
dead grow tired of me and so do I. No path
but to blow out the candle. My ghosts, we
remain, we boast our berth, we duly pray.

And here I begin to begin again, lest
I believe history is abridged at a pulse's end. Our,
we, us—I could fall in love again with family, feet
in the river of my grandpa's scream, and stray
from fearing a man who screamed before fleeing from
his feelings. A man married to love itself. The
whole of him I hold in light-glutted places:
my palm-vase, my eyes' two dusks, our
shared dictum and decree that God
is a woman with a blood-bloomed brain where
twice light entered and photosynthesized. We
can revise this dominion of a stroke met
up with the holy garden of her psyche. Thee
I sing unto, Lord of blood and blossom, lest
my own body confuse its pulse with the seasons, our
covenant that I may believe in what hearts,
many-chambered figs whose wine I grow drunk
from, can accomplish: twin-bell resonance with
another, the chime of two gold rings, the
television's light reflected off their curves, wine
anointing the rings of our mouths. Of
Thee I sing, Lord of Light pouring from the
curve of Grandma's smile, reflecting the world
back at me, me back at me, we
back at we, back to her holding my hand. Forget?
How can I forget her, the gift of life, O Thee?

Cover your head when you visit the dead: Shadowed
beneath grief-need, visit them, but cover up. Beneath

our hunger for their love lies a feast for them, thy
will not their own. Visit them, but clean your hand

before rubbing their grave's dirt. Cover your tracks. May
you carry protection and these words of wisdom: We

are visitors always in the realm of forever.
Don't stand too long near moving water, stand

still at the scent of familiar cologne of a dead true
love. Cover your tracks with sea salt, bathe to

white noise in a white bath: goat's milk and white rose. Our
dead who are our dead will not be afraid. God-

light be with the dark. Don't betray what is true:
You don't miss them as much as they miss you. To

your dead come clean, come ready to work, our
time is not their time, our land no longer native

to they who have closed the circle: land, air, water, fire, land.

NOTES

"The Thirteenth Amendment" takes its inspiration from the 1968 case *Jones v. Alfred H. Mayer Co.*, where Jones, a Black man, charged that the realty company Alfred H. Mayer Company, based in St. Louis, Missouri, discriminated against him by refusing to sell him a home in a particular neighborhood because of his race. The Supreme Court had to decide if the defendant had indeed violated 42 U.S.C. 1982, an act guaranteeing equal rights in purchasing real estate. *Oyez* notes: "The Court sided with Jones and held that Section 1982 of the congressional act was intended to prohibit all discrimination against blacks in the sale and rental of property, including governmental and private discrimination. Furthermore, the Thirteenth Amendment's enforcement section empowered Congress to eliminate racial barriers to the acquisition of property since those barriers constituted 'badges and incidents of slavery.'" For more insight, see "The Thirteenth Amendment and Equal Educational Opportunity" by Brence D. Pernell, published in *Yale Law & Policy Review* 39, no. 2 (2021): 420.

"While Reading *The Orchard*" is for the late Brigit Pegeen Kelly.

"Paradise [Let there be light and Leontyne Price]" is written after "Kintsugi" by Shinji Moon.

"Paradise [Angels dream in cocoons and when hatched]" takes its inspiration from the Japanese animated series *Haibane Renmei*, where angels are born from cocoons and named after the dreams they had therein. Lionel Giles's translation of Sun Tzu's *The Art of War* was consulted for the excerpt.

"Paradise [If I remove myself from this world maybe]" is for the people of Congo, Palestine, Sudan, and . . .

"Paradise [We read about war and wonder]" is written after Mahmoud Darwish's poem "In This Hymn."

"'Til Earth and Heaven Ring" takes its inspiration from the Black National Anthem, "Lift Every Voice and Sing," written as a poem-made-hymn by James Weldon Johnson, later the leader of the NAACP, in 1900. His brother, John Rosamond Johnson, composed the music. The poem is a "golden shovel" using the lyrics of the hymn. According to *Britannica*, a "golden shovel [is] a poetic form in which a line from a pre-existing poem is used to create a new one. Essentially, each word from the borrowed line becomes the last word of each line in the new poem. The form was invented by American poet Terrance Hayes."

ACKNOWLEDGMENTS

AGNI: "The Head of Goliath"

Bennington Review: "Paradise [Assassinate the stars by granting time is ersatz]"

Faultline: "Sculptor and Clay"

Kenyon Review: "Aide-mémoire," "Pastoral, Notwithstanding," "The Lengthening and Shortening of Shadow"

The Missouri Review: "While Reading *The Orchard*" (as "The Fawn")

Muzzle: "Too High"

Obsidian: "While Reading Melvin Dixon"

The Paris-American: "Cascade"

Poetry: "While Reading *Sula*"

Southern Indiana Review: "Paradise [Angels dream in cocoons and when hatched]" and "White Bath"

The Yale Review: "Paradise [We read about war and wonder]" and "While Reading Lucille Clifton"

Zócalo: "The Difficulty of Describing Loneliness"

PHILLIP B. WILLIAMS is the author of the novel *Ours* and two collections of poetry: *Thief in the Interior*, which was the winner of the Kate Tufts Discovery Award and a Lambda Literary Award, and *Mutiny*, which was a finalist for the PEN/Voelcker Award for Poetry Collection and the winner of a 2022 American Book Award. Williams is also the recipient of a Whiting Award and fellowships from the Radcliffe Institute for Advanced Study at Harvard University and the National Endowment for the Arts. Raised in Chicago, he is currently a professor of creative writing at Rice University and is a founding faculty member of the Randolph College low-residency MFA.

PENGUIN POETS

GAROUS ABDOLMALEKIAN
Lean Against This Late Hour

PAIGE ACKERSON-KIELY
Dolefully, A Rampart Stands

JOHN ASHBERY
Selected Poems
Self-Portrait in a Convex Mirror

PAUL BEATTY
Joker, Joker, Deuce

JOSHUA BENNETT
Owed
The Sobbing School
The Study of Human Life
We (the People of the United States)

TED BERRIGAN
The Sonnets

LAUREN BERRY
The Lifting Dress

JOE BONOMO
Installations

PHILIP BOOTH
Lifelines: Selected Poems 1950–1999
Selves

JIM CARROLL
Fear of Dreaming: The Selected Poems
Living at the Movies
Void of Course

SU CHO
The Symmetry of Fish

ADRIENNE CHUNG
Organs of Little Importance

RIO CORTEZ
Golden Ax

MARISSA DAVIS
End of Empire

ALISON HAWTHORNE DEMING
Genius Loci
Rope
Stairway to Heaven

CARL DENNIS
Another Reason
Callings
Earthborn
Earthly Virtues
New and Selected Poems 1974–2004
Night School
Practical Gods
Ranking the Wishes
Unknown Friends

DIANE DI PRIMA
Loba

STUART DISCHELL
Backwards Days
Dig Safe

STEPHEN DOBYNS
Velocities: New and Selected Poems 1966–1992

EDWARD DORN
Way More West

HEID E. ERDRICH
Little Big Bully

ROGER FANNING
The Middle Ages

ADAM FOULDS
The Broken Word: An Epic Poem of the British Empire in Kenya, and the Mau Mau Uprising Against It

CARRIE FOUNTAIN
Burn Lake
Instant Winner
The Life

AMY GERSTLER
Dearest Creature
Ghost Girl
Index of Women
Is This My Final Form?
Medicine
Nerve Storm
Scattered at Sea

EUGENE GLORIA
Drivers at the Short-Time Motel
Hoodlum Birds
My Favorite Warlord
Sightseer in This Killing City

DEBORA GREGER
In Darwin's Room

ZEINA HASHEM BECK
O

TERRANCE HAYES
American Sonnets for My Past and Future Assassin
Hip Logic
How to Be Drawn
Lighthead
So to Speak
Wind in a Box

NATHAN HOKS
The Narrow Circle

ROBERT HUNTER
Sentinel and Other Poems

MARY KARR
Viper Rum

W. B. KECKLER
Sanskrit of the Body

JACK KEROUAC
Book of Blues
Book of Haikus
Book of Sketches

JOANNA KLINK
Circadian
Excerpts from a Secret Prophecy
The Nightfields
Raptus

JOANNE KYGER
As Ever: Selected Poems

ANN LAUTERBACH
Door
Hum
If in Time: Selected Poems 1975–2000
On a Stair
Or to Begin Again
Spell
Under the Sign

PENGUIN POETS

CORINNE LEE
Plenty
Pyx

PHILLIS LEVIN
May Day
Mr. Memory & Other Poems

PATRICIA LOCKWOOD
Motherland Fatherland Homelandsexuals

WILLIAM LOGAN
Rift of Light

J. MICHAEL MARTINEZ
Museum of the Americas
Tarta Americana

ADRIAN MATEJKA
The Big Smoke
Map to the Stars
Mixology
Somebody Else Sold the World

AMBER McBRIDE
Thick with Trouble

MICHAEL McCLURE
Huge Dreams: San Francisco and Beat Poems

ROSE McLARNEY
Colorfast
Forage
Its Day Being Gone

DAVID MELTZER
David's Copy: The Selected Poems of David Meltzer

TERESA K. MILLER
Borderline Fortune

ROBERT MORGAN
Dark Energy
Terroir

CAROL MUSKE-DUKES
Blue Rose
An Octave Above Thunder: New and Selected Poems
Red Trousseau
Twin Cities

ALICE NOTLEY
Being Reflected Upon
Certain Magical Acts
Culture of One
The Descent of Alette
Disobedience
For the Ride
In the Pines
Mysteries of Small Houses

WILLIE PERDOMO
The Crazy Bunch
The Essential Hits of Shorty Bon Bon

DANIEL POPPICK
Fear of Description

LIA PURPURA
It Shouldn't Have Been Beautiful

LAWRENCE RAAB
The History of Forgetting
Visible Signs: New and Selected Poems

BARBARA RAS
The Last Skin
One Hidden Stuff

M.S. REDCHERRIES
mother

MICHAEL ROBBINS
Alien vs. Predator
The Second Sex
Walkman

PATTIANN ROGERS
Flickering
Generations
Holy Heathen Rhapsody
Quickening Fields
Wayfare

SAM SAX
Madness

ROBYN SCHIFF
Information Desk: An Epic
A Woman of Property

WILLIAM STOBB
Absentia
Nervous Systems

MAKSHYA TOLBERT
Shade is a place

TRYFON TOLIDES
An Almost Pure Empty Walking

VINCENT TORO
Hivestruck
Tertulia

PAUL TRAN
All the Flowers Kneeling

SARAH VAP
Viability

ANNE WALDMAN
Gossamurmur
Kill or Cure
Manatee/Humanity
Mesopotopia
Trickster Feminism

JAMES WELCH
Riding the Earthboy 40

PHILIP WHALEN
Overtime: Selected Poems

PHILLIP B. WILLIAMS
Lift Every Voice
Mutiny

MIA S. WILLIS
the space between men

ROBERT WRIGLEY
Anatomy of Melancholy and Other Poems
Beautiful Country
Box
Earthly Meditations: New and Selected Poems
Lives of the Animals
Reign of Snakes
The True Account of Myself as a Bird

MARK YAKICH
The Importance of Peeling Potatoes in Ukraine
Spiritual Exercises
Unrelated Individuals Forming a Group Waiting to Cross